WOULD YOU RATHER?

Also by Richard Herring

Emergency Questions:
1001 Conversation Savers for Every Occasion

The Problem With Men

RICHARD HERRING'S

WOULD YOU RATHER?

SPHERE

SPHERE

First published in Great Britain in 2021 by Sphere
This paperback edition published by Sphere in 2022

3 5 7 9 10 8 6 4 2

A CIP catalogue record for this book
is available from the British Library.

ISBN 978-0-7515-8573-5

Typeset in Bembo by M Rules
Printed and bound in Great Britain by
Clays Ltd, Elcograf S.p.A.

Papers used by Sphere are from well-managed forests
and other responsible sources.

MIX
Paper from
responsible sources
FSC® C104740

Sphere
An imprint of
Little, Brown Book Group
Carmelite House
50 Victoria Embankment
London EC4Y 0DZ

An Hachette UK Company
www.hachette.co.uk

www.littlebrown.co.uk

For Tony Brennan, who kicked this whole thing off for me.

WOULD YOU RATHER?

INTRODUCTION

Would you rather have a fun and playful conversation or sit there in awkward silence, praying to be saved by an alien invasion?

If you've chosen the first option, then congratulations! This is the book for you. It's full of hundreds of conversation starters that should help you delve deep into the psyche of whomsoever you share them with, and hopefully laugh with them too.

If you went for option two . . . come on, mate, lighten up. Have a go and see if you feel a bit better about everything!

The game of 'Would You Rather?' is as old as conversation itself. Ever since the first caveman asked his friend, 'Would you rather be eaten by a pterodactyl or fall into a volcano?' human beings have been posing and ruminating over surreal, morally challenging or simply ridiculous hypothetical questions to pass the time.

It's as much fun to give people a choice between two trickily similar options as it is to confound them with picking a favourite between scenarios that would never usually be compared. In some way, those answers can be the most revealing. They can almost be a kind of therapy*.

I know a bit about asking people weird and unexpected questions, as that's become a significant portion of my interview-based show Richard Herring's Leicester Square Theatre Podcast†. It's been amazing to see how asking people questions that they have never before considered can lead to them opening up and revealing all kinds of things about themselves, even if it is just that they'd prefer to have a time-travelling finger over a nipple that can dispense talcum powder.

There aren't many rules to 'Would You Rather?' but there is additional fun in seeking clarification on the exact parameters of each scenario. In this book I will give you occasional guidelines, but you are welcome to ignore my suggestions and make up your own laws. You will probably be forced to improvise at some point as people are bound to come up with issues that you

---

* Please do not use these in therapy. If your therapist asks you any of these questions then get a new therapist.
† The cool kids call it RHLSTP.

and I haven't previously considered.

Take this classic RHLSTP 'Would You Rather?' question.

Would you rather have a hand made out of ham or an armpit that dispenses sun cream?

It would be a bold interviewee who can leap into an answer for that one without requiring any qualification. And obviously the question leads to all kinds of questions in return:

- If I eat the ham hand, will it grow back?
- What kind of ham are we talking about?
- Can I eat it if I am vegetarian, as it is technically not an animal product?
- Does the hand operate like a regular hand?

And then putting the ham hand to one side:

- How much sun cream are we talking about?
- What factor would it be?
- Would I be able to control the sun cream production or does it spray or ooze out when I am not expecting it?

These became my NB guidelines for the question:

- The ham hand would be a fully operational hand.
- The ham hand will grow back at about the rate of fingernails if you nibble it, but if you eat the whole thing, it will take a month to repair itself, during which time you won't have that particular hand.
- I believe the ham hand is vegan because no animal is involved in its production and nobody dies, but this is your own moral choice.
- You can choose what kind of ham you're going to get before the hand is first installed, but then you have to live with that decision. No changing to Parma ham once you've plumped for breaded.
- The sun cream produced will be enough to cater for reasonable use for you and your immediate family every year, so not enough for it to be a commercial enterprise where you bottle and sell it.
- You will be able to select the factor of the sun cream before your first squirt,

but once selected you cannot change that factor.

- There will be a nozzle in your armpit so the sun cream will only come out when you want it to.

Even though I asked this same question dozens of times I could still be surprised by my guests' follow-ups. David Mitchell wondered if the ham hand would leave a hammy residue on everything one touched with it. I had to think up the rule for that on the spot, deciding that yes it would, but you could wear a little plastic glove like they have on supermarket deli counters if that bothered you.

So, good 'Would You Rather?' questions develop in a collaborative way and the questioner has to be ready to become the questioned. You may wish to make notes in the margin once your own rules have been established or you might want to change the rules every time you ask a question. As with everything in this book, it's very much about your own personal preference.

An equally fun way to play is to only reveal extra details to the question once the respondent has answered. I call these BTWs and will suggest a few throughout the book.

For example:

Would you rather live in the waxy ear of a grumpy giant, eating only what flies in there by accident and not being able to make a noise for fear of being ejected with a huge cotton bud, or live in Middlesbrough?

- BTW The ear wax would be edible and would taste of your favourite food and have zero calories.
- BTW If you choose the latter option you'd live in a mansion with a swimming pool and a yearly sum of £10 million pounds paid into your bank account, but you'd still live in Middlesbrough.

Of course you are welcome to improvise your own BTWs. In this way the game becomes playable over and over again even with the same person.

As long as you're happy with the occasional mention of poo and bottoms then this book is suitable for all ages. The questions may be family-friendly, but your answers don't have to be. I have no control over your imagination. Would you rather I did?

So would you rather turn the page or go on a balloon ride over a snowy mountain?

The choice is yours ... Though of course in this case it's possible to do both. Do send me a photo if you manage it.

Would you rather have a sense of smell that could travel in time (ie you could smell any environment from the past or the future) or have a free pineapple delivered to your door every day for the rest of your life?

NB you will only be able to smell things in the past and future and not interact in any way, and other smells in the vicinity may encroach on your ability to, for example, smell King Henry VIII's fart*.

The pineapple delivery service will be able to find you wherever in the world you are and the fresh whole pineapple will be delivered at 7:00 each morning (though left outside your door and you won't be woken up).

---

* If that was your first thought of what you'd be able to do with this power then have a good, long, hard look at yourself and your priorities.

Would you rather
be the world's worst
shepherd or the
world's only talking
sheep?

**If you had to be a
piece of fruit, what
kind of fruit would
you rather be?**

Would you rather have your entire life broadcast live on TV or live alone in a cave, up a mountain, never visited by anyone?

NB Every incident in your life would be broadcast and you wouldn't be able to block the camera, but it's unlikely that that many people would watch it. But probably at least one person would be watching at all times and you might well know them personally.

The cave would have a decent supply of food and internet access, though it might be dodgy in windy weather.

Would you rather have world peace or £10,000 in your personal bank account, tax free?

If you choose £10,000, how about if it was only £5000? £1000? What's the lowest amount?

If you choose world peace, how much money would it take to change your answer?

Would you rather have the ability to produce honey from a special honey stomach or be able to make a pearl in your kidney every ten years?

NB You would sick the honey up through your mouth, producing 1kg of honey per day, which you could eat, or sell to unsuspecting members of the public.

Each pearl would be worth £8000, but you would have to pass it with your urine via your urethra.

Would you rather be Prince William or Prince Harry?

Would you rather be Kate Middleton or Meghan Markle?

Would you rather
be a tennis ball or
a tennis racket?

**Would you rather have
constantly wet socks or have a
hundred keys on your key ring
and the one you needed was
always the hundredth one you
tried?**

Would you rather have a Swiss Army hand or an Inspector Gadget helicopter blade that emerged from your head?

NB Your hand would have five different Swiss Army knife tools of your choice (instead of your fingers and thumb) but no longer work very effectively as a hand – you would have the choice of which hand it replaced.

The Inspector Gadget helicopter blades would cause you twenty seconds of intense pain every time they emerged from your skull but it wouldn't really hurt on the way back in. Weird, huh?

Would you rather be married to King Henry VIII* or be in the Charge of the Light Brigade?

Would you rather be able to (safely) witness the Big Bang or be always able to find your keys, wallet and personal possessions straight away when you're leaving the house?

---

* In spite of his flatulence.

Would you rather be entombed alive with a dead Pharaoh, but you'd have food, an iPad and a charger and internet access, or have your feet replaced with foot-shaped jellies that were completely incapable of carrying out the necessary functions of feet?

Would you rather be the most famous and successful person of all time, but only after you've died, or get two-for-one meals at Harvester for the rest of your life?

Would you rather
be able to correctly
answer any general
knowledge question
that you're ever
asked or have
everyone think you're
cool?

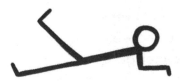

Would you rather go on a cruise
with Tom Cruise or a walking
holiday with Christopher Walken?

Would you rather be the most beautiful person in the world or the cleverest person in the world?

NB If you choose cleverness then your current attractiveness will decrease 25% and if you choose beauty you will become 25% less intelligent.

Would you rather have to live the rest of your life with Emu from Rod Hull and Emu grafted on to your arm and you have to keep him moving and reacting at all times, even when you're on your own (he can sleep when you sleep), or have to have a full bath every day and once it was over have to drink all the bath water before you're allowed to do anything else?

NB If you are too young to remember Rod Hull and Emu you are allowed to Google them before giving your answer.

Would you rather eat a full Christmas dinner for every meal, every day, or eat a medium-sized Easter egg every two hours for the rest of your life?

NB You'd have to finish the Christmas dinner each time, the amount of food on each plate would be ratified by an independent Christmas-dinner expert to be of average Christmas-dinner size and they'd also determine what items were in the dinner.

You'd still have to eat the Easter eggs at night time so would need to set your alarm to go off every two hours. You would not be required to eat the sweets that come with the Easter egg, only the egg itself, but you could eat the sweets if you were hungry. You would be allowed to eat other food if you wished.

Would you rather be the first person on Mars, have life support and food, but no means of returning home, or have everyone know that you were the person who played Jar Jar Binks in those Star Wars films?

Would you rather be imprisoned for a murder that you didn't commit or for a murder that you did commit?

Would you rather have to run ten kilometres right now without stopping, or not?

Would you rather own a car with Jimmy Carr, a lorry with Laurie Anderson or a van with Van Morrison?

Would you rather have the legs of a dog or the face of a turkey?

NB Obviously your arms would be dog legs too, but at least you wouldn't have the face of a turkey.

You wouldn't be able to walk on all fours with your dog legs, but would have to do your best to totter around on the back two and you clearly wouldn't have hands.

Would you rather have to always wash your clothes in a dishwasher or always wash your plates, pans, cups, etc in a washing machine?

NB You'd have to use the dishwasher capsules in the dishwasher and laundry tablets in your washing machine.

You can still use the dishwasher for dishes if you choose to wash your clothes there and your clothes in the washing machine if you do your dishes there.

Would you rather have a conversation with a dolphin or an elephant?

Would you rather have a phone that always had full battery power or have your favourite chocolate bar contain zero calories?

Would you rather have an extra thumb on each hand or be able to shoot poo out of your bum like a cannon?

NB The thumbs would be on the opposite side of your hands to your original thumbs and give you all kinds of advantages when it comes to opening or manipulating objects. You can actually purchase mechanical extra thumbs that you operate with your feet (I am serious), but these ones would be actual extra thumbs. You could hitchhike in two different directions with just one hand!

You wouldn't be able to cause any destruction with the poo cannon, but if someone was hit with the poo, they would get poo on them. But it would also just be fun as a sort of scatological firework show or a tribute at a funeral.

Would you rather be the Man Without a Face or the Man in the Iron Mask?

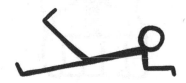

Would you rather spend a night in a haunted house or an afternoon in Middlesbrough?

Would you rather be a horse chestnut tree or an apple tree?

Would you rather be emperor of the shrimps, king of the penguins or queen of the bees?

Would you rather have real-live VAR (the controversial virtual assistant referee used in football matches) so you could play back any argument or incident and find out what exactly was said and who was in the right or wrong (with an independent arbitrator making each decision), or only be able to earn a living as a lookalike of someone famous?

NB Although you would be allowed to style your hair and wear appropriate clothes, you would not be able to change your face to look like a famous person. You would have to choose the famous person you think you most resemble and then only be employable as their lookalike. You can't change your initial decision even if in later years you start to resemble someone else or if you are much too old to be the person you chose.

Would you rather
have a snooty
butler or a slightly
unpredictable chef?

If you had to live in a historical empire, which of the empires would you rather live in?

Would you rather be perfectly fossilised at death and displayed in a future museum as the only example of humanity, but you died on the toilet, or be the emperor of your country, but have been conned into being naked all the time by a salesman who persuades you to wear 'clothes' that only very clever people can see?

Would you rather it turned out we were all just characters in a video game being played by a slightly bored teenager or that the last ten years of your life have just been a dream and you're about to wake up back where you were a decade ago?

Would you rather be happy, grumpy, sleepy, bashful, sneezy, dopey or some kind of unspecified doctor?

Would you rather find a magical land by walking through the back of your wardrobe or by being caught up in a tornado?

Would you rather always be slightly too cold or always be flabbergasted?

Would you rather be shipwrecked for six months or live in an igloo for the next decade?

NB You'd have to survive on the desert island and capture your own food and make your own shelter, but it'd be nice and warm.

The igloo would be as near to your current home as possible so you could still go to work etc, but you wouldn't be allowed in your current home. You could keep your stuff in the igloo but it's not a big igloo.

What would you rather have named after you – the public toilet in the centre of your town or an embarrassing disease?

BTW The toilets would have a big neon sign above them which would have 'The *YOUR NAME* Toilets' on it.

The embarrassing disease would be mentioned on the news a lot and be caught by about one in four people. Realistically you would also have to be the first person to have the disease for it to carry your name. If you have a common name you might be able to convince people that it wasn't you. I can't say in a family book what part of the body your disease affects, but I can confidently predict that it's the part of the body you are currently thinking about.

Would you rather have a tongue that doubled up as a 150cm measuring tape (though one end would always be attached to your throat) or have to drink all your drinks using Henry VI's arm bone as a straw?

Would you rather be dead but not forgotten or forgotten but not dead?

Would you rather know the truth but always have to lie or be really good at ice hockey?

If you had the power to bring one historical figure back to life, out of all the people in history who would you rather reanimate?

Would you rather have antlers or be able to blend into any background like a human chameleon?

BTW The antlers would give you magic powers, allowing you to cavort with woodland sprites on every full moon.

The chameleon powers would be so effective that you often get bumped into or squashed.

Would you rather be Bach or Beethoven?

BTW I mean Beethoven the dog from the 1990s movie franchise. I do mean Bach the composer though, specifically Johann Sebastian, not any of his rubbish children.

Would you rather
get into geological
research or have a nap?

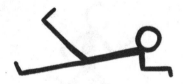

**Would you rather be a
moth or a myth?**

Would you rather spend all your money on whisky and beer or spend most of your money on whisky and beer, but save enough to buy a lottery ticket each week and to buy a Pot Noodle every other day?

Would you rather get to the Olympics by being the person who operates the broom in the curling or by being in the pentathlon but you don't know how to swim or fence?

Which cooking utensil
would you rather be?

**If you could be any element
on the periodic table, which
element would you rather be?**

Would you rather have to keep two raw shelled eggs in your cheeks at all times or have a jaw made of glass?

BTW The glass would be the fragile kind used to make thin wine glasses, not the reinforced kind that can stop a bullet.

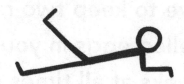

Would you rather have
a hand that is always
covered in ants or
have a family of mice
nesting in your armpit?

Would you rather be a catalyst or have to list all the cats?

Would you rather find the Lost Continent of Atlantis or find a way to tax oxygen and get 10% of all revenue created?

Would you rather own
the Basel Paper Mill
or the Derwent Pencil
Museum?

**Would you rather be a
microbiologist or a biologist of
normal size?**

If you had to wear an item of medieval clothing every day for the rest of your life, would you rather wear an ostentatious ruff or pointy shoes with 30cm long toes?

Would you rather live in a society ruled by children aged six and under or have to be tied to the wheel at a watermill and be spun round for the next thirteen hours?

NB If you choose the water wheel your head will only be underwater for about thirty seconds of each revolution. But it will be very sunny and you won't be allowed suncream or to be released from the waterwheel to go to the toilet.

The children would carry on ruling society for at least five years, maybe more if they do a better job than the current lot.

Would you rather save Venice from ever flooding, but Birmingham is now under three feet of water at all times, or sink Venice, but refloat the *Titanic* and bring all the people who perished when the ship sank back to life?

NB The people of Birmingham would not be allowed to leave their watery city.

Would you rather have free will or own *Free Willy* on DVD?

What would you rather throw at a wall: a very ripe tomato, a watermelon, a coconut, or something of your own choosing?

BTW Whatever you have just chosen to throw will be thrown at you at some point in the next month when you're not expecting it. It's too late to change your mind, I just thought you'd like to know.

Phoebe's Questions

Would You Rather is really for everyone from 6 (and maybe younger) to 106 (but NO ONE OLDER. If any 107-year-olds want to play tell them THEY CAN'T). I have really had fun playing it with my daughter Phoebe, asking her to come up with questions and then debating which option we'd prefer. She basically comes up with hers the same way I do with mine, looking at her immediate environment and then using something she sees to get started, but after a while the questions will get surreal or silly or (more often) go towards the toilet.

I will include some of my daughter's questions now as a little break from mine and, rest assured, I will not be paying her for her work, but offsetting the next few pages against the thousands of pounds she has cost me. I will see you in court, Phoebe Herring.

Would you rather be twenty
feet tall or one foot tall?

Would you rather be zero feet tall or infinity feet tall?

Would you rather be a funfair or a park?

Would you rather be a tree or a leaf?

What would you rather find at the end of the Universe: Candyland or Pink, Purple and Pinky Purple Land?

NB Candyland is obviously a land where everything is made out of sweets, though we did get into a discussion about which things in the land would need to be made of non-candy materials. Phoebe's favourite colours are pink, purple and pinky purple so that land would be things solely based on that limited range of the spectrum. Maybe things can be made out of candy there too to make the choice harder, but there's also the philosophical discussion to be had about whether having nothing but confection would be a heaven or hell. We had a fun chat about what is beyond the edge of the Universe and then what comes after these lands.

Would you rather be the floor or the sky?

Would you rather be an astronaut or a meteorite?

Would you rather be a dragon or a dragonfly?

NB Though again the choice seems obvious, there was the proviso that dragons do not exist so by wishing to be one you might no longer be alive.

Would you rather be a
nose or an eye?

If you had to be a poo, what type of poo would you rather be?

Would you rather be a raindrop or a sundrop?

NB A sundrop is like a raindrop, but it's boiling hot and will burn everything that it falls on! Phoebe would rather be a sundrop.

Would you rather only be able to communicate by the medium of charades or only be able to move around by doing cartwheels?

If you could produce art in the style of any artist throughout history, which artist's work would you rather be capable of producing?

Without Googling, would you rather live in Qeqertaq in Greenland or Zhangjiakou Shi Xuanhua Qu in China?

Would you rather be locked down or locked up?

Would you rather be a diplomat, own a laundromat or have a very nice bathmat?

Would you rather be a *Taskmaster* series champion or a *House of Games* Champion of Champions?*

---

* I mean surely you'd have to be some kind of god to be both

Would you rather float like a butterfly, sting like a bee or lay 40,000 eggs in a day like a queen termite?

Would you rather have one marshmallow right now or wait fifteen minutes and get a bag of marshmallows?

Would you rather be able to understand Quantum Theory or have a social life?

Would you rather lather your father, bother your brother, blister your sister or have another mother?

NB the person answering the question must decide without prompting for themselves if 'another mother' means a different one or an additional one. You will thus gain a valuable insight into their psyche.

Would you rather a roaming chicken laid fresh eggs at your door every morning or an eagle dropped a fresh coconut down your chimney at noon?

Would you rather your first name was Tuppence or Moon Unit?

Would you rather blame it on the sunshine, the moonlight, the good times or the boogie?

If you were going to be in a race, would you rather be a tortoise or a hare? I know that the tortoise won that one time, but come on, how likely is that to happen again? Especially now all hares must know what happened.

Would you rather be
immoral or amoral?

Would you rather compete
at Wimbledon but you're not
allowed to practise tennis
beforehand or have to sing all
the verses of the UK National
Anthem at the FA Cup Final
without being allowed to look
up the lyrics or have singing
lessons?

Would you rather have to have jalapeños or anchovies in every meal you eat from now on?

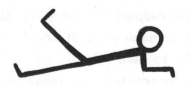

If you had the power to stop one disaster would you rather prevent the Great Fire of London or the volcanic eruption that destroyed Pompeii?

NB by altering history you would almost certainly change things so much that you will never be born, but you have to make the choice either way.

There are a few facts to balance: the numbers of casualties in Pompeii was significantly higher than in London, but modern day Pompeii is very reliant on tourism (and the volcano has left an incredible trove of finds for archaeologists). Also, in many ways the Great Fire of London paved the way for a more efficient modern city and may have helped eradicate the plague. Don't just make an arbitrary decision. You have to save one city and in doing so destroy yourself, so please think carefully.

Would you rather be sent to Coventry or have the scent of Coventry?

Would you rather have a small painless wart on your forehead or a huge sore wart on your bottom?

NB The warts cannot be removed but will fall off naturally after five years.

If you could make an ice cream or lolly out of any sweet or confectionery that currently doesn't have an ice cream or lolly version, which sweet or confection would you rather transform into a lolly or ice cream?

NB If you choose something that unbeknownst to you already has an ice cream or lolly version you lose twenty points. As this is the only question that has points involved then you have now lost the game.

If you could change one thing about the human body, which one thing would you rather change?

Which Mr Man or Little Miss would you rather be?

Would you rather be a dung beetle and only eat dung or a burrowing owl whose main diet is dung beetles?

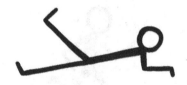

Would you rather be always underdressed or always overdressed?

If you could make one part of your body or one of your senses fifty times more sensitive than it currently is, which body part or sense would get a fifty times increase in sensitivity?

Would you rather have 10,000 spoons when all you need is a knife or be able to fully understand irony?

Would you rather be unable to sweat or only allowed to eat in Pizza Express in Woking?

Would you rather have a top knot or a tonk pot?

NB A tonk pot is a pot that you can tonk in.

Would you rather live on beetle juice or live on Betelgeuse?

BTW Although Betelgeuse is a star you'd be given special shoes that would mean you could live there without being burned up. You would however be alone and have nothing to eat except whatever stars are made of. But it still might be better than living on liquidised beetles.

BTW the beetle that would be juiced would always be a dung beetle.

Would you rather be an exhibit in an alien zoo, have all your needs catered for, but live in a cage and be gawped at daily, or live in an alien safari park where you would have freedom to roam, but would have to avoid super-rich aliens who have paid to hunt you and want to put your head on their wall?

Would you rather have to sleep in a skip for a week or skip a week's sleep?

Would you rather teach an old dog new tricks or teach an old dog to add a bit of pizzazz to its old tricks?

Would you rather prevent harm to a farmer or a pharmacist?

Would you rather have the power to administer a debilitating electric shock or be able to squirt ink from your bottom so you could thwart attackers whilst making your escape?

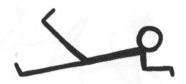

Would you rather go to the dump for an afternoon or get a visitation from an angel who immediately realises they've appeared to the wrong person and then disappears before you can get a camera?

Would you rather be painted by Leonardo da Vinci or have a song written about you by Paul McCartney?

If you had to be a superhero with the power of an insect (that has not yet been taken by another superhero) which radioactive insect would you rather had bitten you?

Would you rather be fair-minded, fare-dodging, fair-haired or at a funfair?

Would you rather have your own personal dental hygienist who only looked after you and your teeth, was on twenty-four-hour call to clean your teeth whenever you liked and came with a fully equipped dental hygiene suite, or be able to lift fifty times your weight?

Would you rather be a professional operatic soprano or have a wasp in your ear that can read people's minds and whisper what they are thinking?

NB The wasp in your ear would buzz fairly consistently and you would need to feed it regularly with spiders and insects. It would never be able to escape the prison in your ear and would eventually die in there.

But being a professional opera singer is a very demanding job and you won't be able to read minds. And you will have to use whatever range you currently have and just hope you can hit the high notes.

Would you rather be King Stephen or Stephen King?

Would you rather be a vampire or a Shrek?

Would you rather
go into suspended
animation and
not wake up for
five years or five
hundred years?

**Would you rather have 'Danger'
as your middle name or have a
species of spider named after
you?**

Would you rather
discover the Lost
Continent of Atlantis or
the Holy Grail?

Would you rather
be Emperor Nero or
Captain Nemo?

**BTW You should put the winner of that
contest up against Neo from the _Matrix_.**

Would you rather discover the bones of an unknown species of dinosaur that would be named after you or buried treasure?

Would you rather pump up the volume or plump up some cushions?

Would you rather be one of the Three Bears or one of the Three Blind Mice?

Would you rather be able to beat God in a fist fight or be able to complete the Rubik's Cube in world record time?

Would you rather be able to always tell when people were lying or carry on with the current system where you have to guess?

NB Always knowing the truth might be worse than being lied to. On the other hand you'd be able to solve a lot of crimes.

Would you rather go to school in Hogwarts or the actual school you went (or go) to?

NB Bear in mind that if you are a muggle, which I am guessing you are, you are going to experience a lot of bullying from the Slytherin kids, plus there's the danger of being killed in battle against (or for) evil, but the sweets are good.

If you could turn back time by thirty minutes, once in your lifetime, would you rather use that power retrospectively now to change something that's already happened or save it up for the future?

Would you rather go ten-pin bowling or ice skating?

Would you rather go ten pin bowling or be the Prime Minister of the Central African Republic?

NB If you were PM of the Central African Republic you would be banned from playing ten pin bowling. Also, if you choose bowling then you are agreeing that you will never be permitted to be Prime Minister of the Central African Republic.

Would you rather play international football for North Macedonia or inherit a chain of struggling burger restaurants that would need you to put in some serious work to make profitable?

NB If you are vegetarian you would be welcome to have the restaurants serve only veggie burgers, in fact that kind of thinking might be what turns things round for you.

Would you rather be a rampaging elephant or a withdrawn otter?

Would you rather be the inventor of a machine that could translate everything a baby was thinking and feeling into words, or an inventor of a machine that would make teenagers polite and unselfish for an hour and a half every day?

Would you rather die
on your feet, live on
your knees or slide
down a bank of snow
on your bottom?

Would you rather be a sword swallower or one of those guys who can spit fire?

Would you rather own a team of talking puppies, who could drive vehicles and act as an emergency service in your town, or a collection of talking trains with faces and personalities, who are able to ferry passengers and freight around, but who sometimes complain about the menial tasks they perform and question who they are, how they came to be anthropomorphised transport and why they are beholden to you?

Would you rather have a free pick 'n' mix display in your home (the contents of which would be refreshed each morning) or unlimited nachos (and all the accoutrements) made for you by a dedicated nacho chef whenever you desired them?

NB You would be within your rights to sell either item to passers-by at hugely inflated prices and however big the mark-up nobody would complain.

Would you rather be swallowed by a whale, but get to live in its belly for three days like Jonah, or have a tapeworm living in you for three months?

Would you rather serve in Heaven or rule in Hell?*

---

* Thanks to John Milton for this excellent question.

If you had a goose that could lay eggs of any material you wished for, but once you'd chosen what it could lay you couldn't change your mind, what kind of eggs would you rather your goose laid?

NB The eggs would always be egg-shaped and goose-egg-sized and composed of only one basic material, but if you wished to have a liquid like printer ink, then you would be allowed to have a shell. You can choose for the egg to be made of egg, but that seems a bit of a waste of the magic goose's powers.

Would you rather travel to an alternate universe where you are 25% happier, richer and have a better job, but you have to kill the alternate version of you to live their life, or be allowed to restart your own life, with everything you already know, but you are born as a random baby anywhere on the planet?

If all the art galleries and museums in the world got together and said they would gift you one item from their combined catalogues, which piece of art or artefact would you rather choose to own?

Would you rather be able to telephone your eight-year-old self and have five minutes to tell them any information that you think might be useful or get a five-word text message from yourself from twenty years in the future?

NB Within the five minutes you would have to convince the eight-year-old you that you were really them and that they should listen to you and remember what you tell them, without your parents getting suspicious about who this mysterious adult was talking to their child.

You would know the text message from the future was genuine but would have to decide if acting upon it would have damaging consequences to the space/ time continuum and also change the circumstances that the future-you was experiencing.

**Would you rather
know how you'll die
or what will happen
to you after you die?**

Would you rather be playing table
tennis or knitting?

Would you rather be playing footgolf or basketballoon?

NB In footgolf you have to kick a golf ball round an eighteen-hole golf course, getting the ball into each hole in turn in the fewest number of kicks.

Basketballoon is like basketball except you use a balloon (inflated with regular air) instead of a ball. You are allowed to replace the balloon if it bursts.

Would you rather have the moon on a stick or a flying pig?

NB Warning – moving the moon around might have huge gravitational repercussions for Planet Earth, but also a flying pig might lead to pig droppings.

Would you rather
be making soap or
be at home with my
Dachshund?

BTW My Dachshund is a snappy little fella.

Would you rather be a reverse mermaid (head and body of a fish, legs of a human) or reverse centaur (head and body of a horse, legs of a human)?

Would you rather fall in love or fall into a swimming pool full of your favourite biscuits?

Would you rather be the best at mental gymnastics or actual gymnastics?

Would you rather suffer from Arachibutyrophobia (fear of peanut butter sticking to the roof of your mouth) or Hippopotomonstro-sesquippedaliophobia (fear of long words)?

BTW How insensitive is it that they made that such a long word?

**If you could be
any puppet, which
puppet would you
rather be?**

Would you rather be nonchalant,
semi-chalant or 100% fully chalant?

Would you rather the Olympics introduced a new form of dressage where the horse had to dance while the rider had a pint of beer on their head and whoever spilled the least beer got the gold medal, or self-playing table tennis in which each player had to keep a rally going as long as possible by running round the table and hitting the ball back to themselves, or a better weird sport of your own invention?

NB You must come up with your own new sport within five seconds of this NB being read out or it doesn't count.

Would you rather eat better or sleep better?

Would you rather be a lion for a day, a panther for nine hours, an ocelot for a fortnight, a squid for three minutes or a hump-backed whale for eight months?

Would you rather do the right thing and lose or the wrong thing and win?

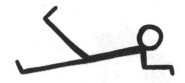

Would you rather give up the rest of your life to attempt to reverse global warming and save the planet, or spend the rest of your life partying like a maniac before attaching booster rockets to Earth and flying it into the sun?

Would you rather live in a giant shoe or a giant peach?

Would you rather lose a kidney or find one?

If you had to add another head to Mount Rushmore, whose head would you rather see carved in stone next to the current four?

Would you rather be
cruel to be kind or be
kind to be kind?

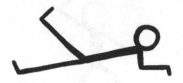

Would you rather be judge, jury and executioner; judge and jury, but not executioner; judge and executioner, but not jury; jury and executioner but not judge; just judge; just jury; or just executioner?

Wouldn't you rather be Hemeling?

NB If you get that reference you are quite old and have a good memory. If you would rather be Hemeling then you are the only person in history who would.

If you had to be a sitcom character which one would you rather be?

NB You would have to live their entire life, both the stuff you've seen on screen and everything else that was never filmed.

Would you rather fight a horse-sized duck or have everyone believe you'd kissed your cousin, even though you hadn't?

Would you rather be a Second World War Prisoner of War trying to escape from confinement or a medieval knight about to go into battle?

Would you rather have all your teeth fall out and be replaced with the teeth of a Neanderthal man (or woman) or have all your hair fall out and be replaced with the wire from a Brillo pad?

NB The Neanderthal teeth would be fitted into your mouth very firmly and work effectively but bear in mind that Neanderthals had large anterior teeth marked by strong shovelling, marked labial convexity, and prominent lingual tubercles, as well as postcanine teeth with enlarged pulp chambers.

Andrew Neil chose the hair option and it seems to have worked out for him.

Would you rather only be able to communicate with the vocabulary of a sat nav or have one very cold hand that you could never get any warmer whatever you did?

NB The hand isn't so cold that it makes it unusable, but it's annoyingly and distractingly cold.

Would you rather have saved the world but nobody knew about it or have done nothing of value but have your face constantly projected on to the moon?

Would you rather have an extra hour every day for the rest of your life that was available only to you or get to be the best player of any sport of your choice for a whole year, but then go back to your current skill level?

Would you rather
inherit the earth,
see God or be
comforted?*

**Would you rather confess all
your sins and be forgiven, but
have everyone know what you'd
done, or have to do all your sins
again, but have no one find out?**

---

* Thanks to Jesus Christ for this excellent question.

Would you rather be
the inventor of the Pop
Tart or of string cheese?

Would you rather have to work as
a living scarecrow every day for ten
years or be used as a human crash
test dummy once a year for the
next decade?

**NB If you choose the crash test dummy
you would regenerate each time you die
and injuries would all immediately heal,
but you'd still experience the pain.**

Would you rather always have to wear clothing covered in sequins or only be allowed to wear grey clothing?

Without looking these words up, would you rather be ultracrepidarian or eximious?

Would you rather always come second or win one in ten times and come last nine in ten times?

Would you rather a bread bin was something that you threw mouldy bread into or somewhere you kept your fresh bread?

Would you rather be bitten by a dog or fall into a sewer?

NB The bite would break skin and require a bandage and take a couple of weeks to heal. You would be pulled out of the sewer straight away, but only after being fully submerged in sewage.

Would you rather be a one-hit wonder with a song that most people find annoying, but that brings in £15,000 a year in royalties, or get to appear as a new character in your favourite TV show for an entire series, but be regarded by many fans as the Scrappy Doo of the show?

NB If your favourite show is _Scooby Doo_ your new character would be Scrappy Doo's more annoying sibling.

Would you rather go on a fortnight skiing holiday with Wee Jimmy Krankie (in character the whole time) or dismantle and then reassemble a car engine with Hunter from *Gladiators*?

**Would you rather
be Britain's oldest
hairdresser or
France's youngest
shepherd?**

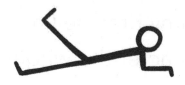

If you could abolish one law, which
law would you rather get rid of?

If you could call yourself by any nickname and everyone else in the world had to call you by that nickname whenever they talked about or to you, what nickname would you rather have?

Would you rather that the moon was literally made of cheese or that little boys were literally made of slugs and snails and puppy dogs' tails?

Adult Questions

Although none of the questions in this book are too rude for kids (apart from the one about bottom burps, but I am a rebel and refuse to take that one out), there are a few that kids might find confusing or boring or refer to things from long before they were born that they have no knowledge or interest in. So, we've decided to make a section that is 'Adults Only' which you are welcome to pretend is full of filth and secrets that the little ones mustn't ever see. Imagine their disappointment when they sneak downstairs at night to read them and discover they're mainly about 1980s TV stars.

Or you can just ask your kids anyway and see how they interpret the questions – it's often fun to have to answer a question that you have absolutely no inkling about. And it will be good practice for if they ever become a politician or TV pundit.

Would you rather have to run every business decision and purchase you make by the Dragons from *Dragons' Den* or spend the rest of your entire working life doing tasks set for you by Sir Alan Sugar*?

---

* (or whoever does *The Apprentice* in your country. Bad luck Americans)

Would you rather have a time machine that can only take you to the 1973 wedding of Princess Anne and Mark Phillips or an invisibility cloak that glitches randomly at least once a minute, making you totally visible for a couple of seconds?

NB You would only be able to travel to the actual wedding ceremony and not be able to leave Westminster Abbey.

You might get lucky and have forty-five seconds of total invisibility, but might appear at any time.

BTW the invisibility cloak only works if you are otherwise totally naked.

Would you rather live in a world
that had no caffeine or no alcohol?

Would you rather
have tea or coffee?

BTW The coffee will shrink you down
to six inches in height for the next
four hours.

The tea will make you slightly
more adept at Sudoku for the next
eighteen minutes.

Would you rather
be able to fart the
Blockbusters' theme
tune or own a cat?

**Would you rather play cricket
with Mike Batt and Johnny
Ball or play golf with Jeremy
Irons and Ronnie Wood?**

Would you rather have Angelina Jolie's lips or Jennifer Aniston's hair?

BTW The lips would not replace your own lips, but be put in the middle of your back. The lips would be autonomous and be able to talk and need feeding and would be furious about being transplanted in your back.

The hair would be all the hair that has ever grown out of Jennifer Aniston's head and body and you wouldn't be able to trim or shave it off. You'd have a lifetime's worth of (admittedly celebrity) hair growing on whatever part of the body it initially grew on (or nearest equivalent).

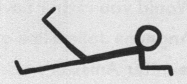

Would you rather be able to automatically distinguish between Chris Pratt, Chris Pine, Chris Evans (US) and Chris Hemsworth with 88% accuracy or just continue living your current existence where you assume they are all the same person?

Would you rather motorcycle
round the world with Charley
Boorman or be imprisoned
in chains in a dungeon for
115 days eating only gruel
and having no toilet facilities
with Ewan McGregor?

Would you rather have an elephant in your room, but no one was allowed to notice or talk about it, or a portrait of yourself in your attic that showed you as if you'd never shaved any of your bodily hair, whilst you yourself would have no bodily hair?

NB Any hair above your neck would not be included in the deal.

The elephant can do amazing tricks, but everyone has to ignore them.

Would you rather ask what your country can do for you or ask what you can do for your country?

Which product that has rebranded and changed its name would you rather see forced to go back to its original name?

Would you rather experience the life of the protagonist of *Quantum Leap* or *Total Recall*? Or a version of *Total Recall* where you were living the life of the protagonist of *Quantum Leap*?

Would you rather live in a world where the film *Yesterday* had never been made or the world in which it had been made?

Would you rather be Putin or Rasputin?

If you had to name your child after a superhero (meaning their superhero name, eg Iron Man) which superhero would you rather your child was named after?

Which failed website or internet start-up company would you rather had succeeded?

Would you rather go to Eton or Grange Hill?

Would you rather be as tall as Richard Osman or have the bank balance of Richard Osman?

Would you rather be in Fight Club, but talk about Fight Club, or be not in Fight Club and never talk about Fight Club and think Fight Club is stupid (but never tell anyone)?

Would you rather get to have one free return First Class Flight to anywhere of your choosing but then never be allowed in First Class again or have every flight you take from now on upgraded to Premium Economy with priority boarding and an extra 2kg of luggage allowance?

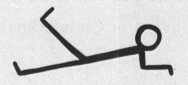

Would you rather be Paul McCartney or John Lennon?

Would you rather be Chris Evans or Chris Evans?

Would you rather that the only milk you were allowed to drink was cat milk or the only biscuits you were allowed to eat were dog biscuits?

BTW You would have to consume at least half a pint of cat milk or eat ten dog biscuits (random brands, so you couldn't just find one that you didn't mind) every day.

Would you rather be a martyr or a tomato?

Would you rather jump a shark or limbo under a zebra?

Would you rather be handcuffed to your worst enemy for a week or be lactose intolerant?

Would you rather be able to live your life again and make three changes or have to relive one random day 100 times, but be able to change anything with no consequences?

If you could wake up in a world where the work of one musician or band had never been created, which body of music would you rather be rid of?

NB And would you get rid of it so you could 'rewrite' all the tunes and take the credit or just so you'd never have to hear it again? Do you think that having done the latter the music still wouldn't play in your mind though? Probably more often than it would if you'd just let things be?

Would you rather be
a pawn or a prawn?

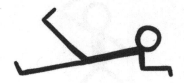

Which of your
childhood toys would
you rather see come to
life?

If you were in a creepy second-hand bookshop and found a weird-looking book that you realised contained the story of your life, from your birth to your death, would you rather see how it ends or find out what presents you're getting for Christmas this year?

Would you rather fall into lava or be eaten by a crocodile?

Would you rather listen to no music
apart from your favourite song
for the rest of your life, or have to
listen to your least favourite song,
on repeat, night and day for the
next year?

**NB Once the year was up, if you had
survived, you would be able to listen to
any music you liked.**

**If you go for your favourite song,
you can listen to it (or not listen to it)
whenever you want, so you can have no
music. But if you want music, it will just
be the one song.**

Would you rather be a barrister or a barista?

Would you rather be able to fluently speak and understand all the languages in the world, or have a priority pass to Legoland for you and three friends which allowed you unlimited free entry to the theme park and to go to the front of every queue and on your birthday you'd get to have the whole place open just for the four of you?

When humans become extinct, which other species of animal would you rather see evolve intelligence and self-awareness next?

Would you rather that everyone in the world believed in the same religion, but had unfortunately chosen the wrong one, or that we continued with the current system where everyone believes different stuff and gets into fights about it, but one lot of people might be right?

If you could rename all
the months of the year,
what names would you
rather we used?

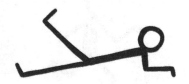

Would you rather
own a Bunsen burner
or an overhead
projector?

Would you rather
make a living writing
hypothetical questions
or have a proper job?

Would you rather never have back pain again or never have a headache again?

Would you rather run a marathon or stay at home and eat a big bowl of ice cream and the ice cream has no calories and eating it actually makes you fitter than doing a marathon and they give you a medal at the end for eating the ice cream and it's nicer than the medal you get for marathons?

If you could only wear one style of trouser/sweat pant/skirt/leg covering for the rest of your life, on all occasions, including in bed, which style of leg covering would you rather wear?

NB You would be able to have more than one pair of whatever you were wearing.

Would you rather have
a theme song that
played every time you
entered a room (and
what would it be?) or
be able to fast forward
twenty minutes once
a day, but only when
you're awake?

**NB There is no guarantee that you
wouldn't miss something important.
You would not be able to see the future
before making your decision about
when to fast forward.**

Would you rather be lord of the flies, earl of the earwigs or duke of the dung beetles?

Would you rather have a foot fungus or edible mushrooms growing out of your ears?

Would you rather be a dandelion or a dandy lion?

If you could choose anyone to be your parents, who would you rather have as your parents?

Would you rather be Walter Raleigh or Francis Drake, or do you think they are the same person?

Would you rather give or receive?

Would you rather eat a whole 250g pack of butter in the next five minutes or have to improvise a twenty-minute speech to the United Nations about how you would create world peace right now?

NB You can't spread the butter on another food or mix it with other ingredients or heat it up and turn it into a delicious drink.

If you fail to eat the butter in five minutes then you have to give the speech anyway, feeling nauseous from consuming maybe 100g or more of butter.

If the UN don't like your speech and think you have failed to come up with a solution to war then they will make you eat 250g of butter in five minutes as a punishment.

So basically I am asking, do you think you can eat a 250g pack of butter in five minutes?

Would you rather count out loud to a million or do 150 press ups?

Would you rather invent a drug that saved loads of lives but you gave to the world for free or a drug that cured no one but made you loads of money?

Would you rather have the smelliest bottom burps in the world but no one knew it was you that was doing them or relatively inoffensive guffs that you were always found out for?

NB The bad trumps would be so bad that even you wouldn't like them, plus even though you'd been reassured you'd never be found out you would surely be nervous that one day someone would make the connection.

Would you rather have to host ITV's *Tipping Point* once a week for the rest of your life or own a canoe?

NB If you already own a canoe, it would be a better canoe than your current canoe.

Would you rather have to bring up a salamander, pretending it was your human baby, without allowing your subterfuge to be discovered, or have to eat only what a salamander eats for a year?

BTW You would be imprisoned for six months if anyone found out that it was a salamander and not a baby, but if you get to one year and no one suspects a thing you win a lifetime's supply of KitKats.

Salamanders eat insects and spiders and pests like slugs and larvae. Also worms and small animals. They sometimes eat other salamanders. You get no KitKats if you complete this task.

Would you rather win Best in Show at the Home-made Marmalade Awards or come third in an untelevised Formula 1 Grand Prix race?

Would you rather appear on a reboot of *Friends* as a new friend of the *Friends* gang, but although the other actors have scripted lines and know what's going to happen, you have to improvise everything and haven't been at rehearsals (the other actors have been told you think that rehearsal is beneath you), or be a new scripted character in *Mrs Brown's Boys*?

Would you rather be a gladiator in Ancient Rome or a Gladiator from the 1990s TV show, but twenty years after the show has finished and you don't get to choose which gladiator?

Would you rather row your boat gently down the stream or boisterously on the crashing waves of the open sea?

Would you rather win
an Olympic medal for
Swingball or the Nobel
Prize for identifying
what other film or TV
programme you've
seen that actor in
before?

Would you rather live in the seventeenth century or the twenty-third century?

NB You don't get to check out the future first. It might be better or it might be much worse.

BTW You would know everything that you know now whichever direction you head in, so depending on what you remember you could be the greatest inventor/philosopher/scientist/author of the 1600s.

Would you rather have a lorry full of Soleros but no way to refrigerate them or a lorry full of Pop Tarts but no way of heating them up?

Would you rather spend the rest of your life playing snooker against yourself in an attic or trying to clear all the stones from a very stony field?

Would you rather have headlights on your forehead or indicators on your bottom?

NB You could cut holes in your trousers or skirt so the indicators could be seen.

Would you rather be able to hover 2cm off the ground, or be able to teleport, but only within a radius of 3ft and you have no control over which direction?

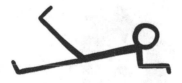

Would you rather have a brain that could connect to Wi-Fi or an immunity to arthritis?

Would you rather that Shrek made an appearance (however fleeting) in every film that has ever been made or that every film (even deadly serious ones) had to star the Muppets with just a handful of parts given to humans?

Would you rather be a lumberjack or a lion tamer?

Would you rather have a pet bee that was the size of a cushion or a pet giraffe that was the size of a large dog?

Would you rather be a mime or one of those people who pretends to be a statue?

Would you rather judge not lest ye be judged or keep on judging and hope no one starts turning their attention on to you?

If you could decommission one TV show, which programme would you rather be rid of?

Would you rather represent the UK in the Eurovision Song Contest or at ski jumping? If you choose ski jumping you forget your kit and though you manage to borrow some skis, you end up having to do it completely naked.

NB Both events are televised live.

Would you rather
have a Wagon Wheel
biscuit as big as an
actual wagon wheel,
a Mars Bar as big as
Mars or a Milky Way
as big as the Milky
Way?

Would you rather have armour and horns like a rhinoceros or spikes and the ability to roll up in a ball like a hedgehog?

Would you rather own a sweet shop or play football for York City FC?

NB However good you were at football you would never be able to change club. York City are, at time of writing, in the National League North.

Would you rather get a thousand emails a day that all demanded an immediate answer or no emails a day?

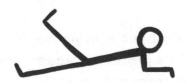

Would you rather you could never treat anything with gravity or that there was no actual gravity?

Would you rather have a magic carpet that could never become dirty whatever was spilled on it or trodden into it, or a magic carpet that if you sat on it could fly you around wherever you wanted to go, but would need to be regularly dry cleaned?

NB Remember the flying magic carpet offers little protection against the weather or the cold or collision with birds.

Would you rather
have a world
without antonyms or
synonyms?

Would you rather be
declined or disinclined?

Would you rather have the latest smartphone but a single charge doesn't even last the day or have one of the 1990s Nokias that only had Snake on it, but the battery lasted ages and it worked as a phone?

Would you rather just be left alone?

Would you rather be *Microtheoris vibicalis*, the whip-marked snout moth, or Armando Manuel, the Angolan politician who was Minister of Finance in Angola from 2013 to 2016?

NB I'll level with you. I write some of these by just pressing the 'random article' button on Wikipedia. I bet no one has ever asked this question before though. Entries about moths come up much more often than you'd think. The next time I pressed it, it came up with *Cryptoblabes alphitias*, which is another breed of snout moth.

Would you rather work at MI5 or MFI?

NB You'd be working at MFI, the furniture retailer, in its heyday back in the 1970s as it is now defunct.

If *Love Island* was just one of a huge series of reality TV shows where people exhibiting the same emotion were put on a small area of land surrounded by sea, would you rather be on Love Island, Hate Island, Anger Island, Embarrassment Island, Happiness Island, Sadness Island, Ennui Island, Excitement Island, Fear Island or an emotion of your own choice Island?

Would you rather
something as good
as this never ended
or had never begun,
so you wouldn't have
the disappointment of
having to bid it adieu?

NB Is it better to have asked would you rather questions and lost, than never to have asked would you rather questions at all?

WOULD YOU RATHER QUESTION GENERATOR

Hey look, I am the first to admit that it's pretty easy to come up with would you rather questions by yourself, but it's not so easy to come up with ones that will spark proper conversations or laughter. I seem to be better than most adults at doing this. We all have our part to play.

BUT I want to help you be as good at this largely useless skill as I am, so for the last few pages I will give you some templates to create even more stupid questions, so that the would–you–rather fun NEVER STOPS. Choose your own words to go in the brackets:

Would you rather be [a body part of an animal] or [a piece of sporting equipment]?

Would you rather kick a [?] or kiss a [?]?

Would you rather eradicate [an emotion] or blow up [a building]?

Would you rather have bigger [?] or build a statue to [person you neither love or hate]?

Would you rather ride a [?] or hide in a [?]?

Would you rather control [type of weather] or invent [a sci-fi technology]?

Would you rather be [James Bond villain] or [Disney Princess]?

Would you rather work for [?] or dive into a pile of [?]?

Would you rather be [name of billionaire] or [Greek god]?

Would you rather that [?] had no [?] or that you could turn [?] into [?]?

ACKNOWLEDGEMENTS

Thanks to Rhiannon Smith, my brilliant editor for suggesting this book in the first place, Thalia Proctor, Louise Harvey, Nico Taylor, Marie Hrynczak and everyone at Sphere.

To Katie McKay, Jon Thoday, Julien Matthews and Jules Lom at Avalon.

To the RHLSTP listeners and especially the monthly badgers. This book belongs to you, but you still have to pay for it and I get all the money for doing it.

To the RHLSTP guests for being the first to answer some of these questions and helping me to work out which ones worked (and which ones didn't).

To the staff of the Lister Hospital Stevenage and Mount Vernon Cancer Centre for ensuring I am still here to make up stupid questions. I am sure that makes all your hard work seem worthwhile!

To Phoebe Herring for her ace questions and for playing this game with me in the car.

To Ernie Herring, who falls outside the 6 to 106 age range and thus MUST NOT PLAY (until 2023, but not after 2124).

To Catherine Herring for everything.

ABOUT THE AUTHOR

Richard Herring has enjoyed phenomenal success as a writer and performer and is an innovator in the world of podcasts. Persistently placing in the Top 10 UK Comedy Podcast chart, *Richard Herring's Leicester Square Theatre Podcast (RHLSTP)* sees him interview top comedians in front of a live audience, with previous guests including Sir Michael Palin, Dawn French and Grayson Perry. He has written and appeared in a number of critically acclaimed plays, is a frequent guest on television panel shows, regularly tours as a stand-up comedian and was the winner of series 10 of *Taskmaster*. He's also won a *House of Games* Champion of Champions trophy. And it only took him four goes to win *Pointless*.

NOTES